A True Story
Bill Gainer

Used Poems, 2003 - 2021

Spartan Press
Kansas City, MO
spartanpress.com

Copyright © Bill Gainer, 2021
First Edition: 1 3 5 7 9 10 8 6 4 2
ISBN: 978-1-952411-69-4
LCCN: 2021943652

Cover photo: Ryan Snellman
Title page photo: Lynn Alexander
Back cover photos: Kat Spencer
All rights reserved. No part of this publication may be reproduced or transmitted in any form or by any means, electronic or mechanical, including photocopying, recording or by info retrieval system, without prior written permission from the author.

Special thanks – Jason Ryberg, John Dorsey, Evan Myquest, Todd Cirillo and the editors of these publications:

Invitation from the Jukebox; a broadside, Rattlesnake Press, 2009, *Antique Children,* 2011, *Medusa's Kitchen,* Epic Rites Press, *The Sacramento News and Review, The Reno News and Review,, The Rattlesnake Review, Beatitude,* Six Ft. Swells Press anthologies: *Cocktails and Confessions, Lost Valentines, The Nevada County Union Newspaper, Poems for All, The Tule Review, Poetry Now, The Crazy Child's Scribbler,* The Beat Museum's website; *thebeatmuseum*.org, *WTF, Heavy Bear, The Chiron Review, Rufous City Review, Sketch Book, Red Fez, Mad Rush Magazine, Guerilla Pamphlets, Green Panda Press, Outlaw Poetry Network, Regardless of Authority, Rusty Truck, Durable Goods, Citizens for Decent Literature, Zygote in my Coffee, Primal Urge Magazine, Chico News and Review, Guide to the Arts, Kiss of Death Press, Zygote in My Fez, The Long Way Home.* Lummox Press, 2009, *Fast Short and Deadly, Magnet Project*: rlcrow. com, *Gasconade Review #6, The Bicycle Review, Zero Percent, Sacramento Voices, Spirit Caller Magazine, Trailer Park Quarterly, Slaves and Bulldozers, Up the Staircase Quarterly, The Advocate, The Huffington Post, A Kiss in Hell, Tree Killer Ink, Bay Area Generations 16, Blotterature, Convergence, Bold Monkey, Full of Crow, In Between Hangovers, Kissing Shadows, Tree Killer Ink 2017, Lummox Journal 3/ 4/ 5/ 6/ 7/ 8, Midnight Lane Boutique, Poet Hound, Poetrybay, Queen Ann's Revenge, Specious Species, Six Ft. Swells Press, The Cutting Room Floor, The Machine, The Naked Bulb Anthology 2016, This is Poetry, Cultural Weekly.*

Roxy. R.L. Crow Publications, 2003
To Run With the Savages. Rattlesnake Press, 2005
The Mysterious Woman Next Door. Lummox Press, 2008
Joining the Demented. Rattlesnake Press, 2009
A Note in the Window. Red Alice Books, 2011
Louisiana Calling. NightBallet Press, 2013
The Fine Art of Poisoning. Red Alice Books, 2013
Lipstick and Bullet Holes. Epic Rights Press, 2014
The Mysterious Book of Old Man Poems. Lummox Press, 2017

*To the lies that keep us together
and the truths that keep us apart.*

Table of Contents

Roxy

Catching Knives with Your Teeth	1
Coffee Shop Blues	2
Separate Goals	3
An Abbott and Costello Love Story	4
Memories of a Romance ...	5
The Touch	6
The Bookstore Clerk	7
Ummm –	8
Whispers in Public	9
Anxiety's Bite	10
That New York Thing	11
It Might As Well Been Written ...	12
The Addict	13
The Gender Police	14
She Answered	15
Her Powder	16

To Run With the Savages

To Run With the Savages	18
The Contender	19
The Visit	20
Invitations from the Jukebox	21
The Emergency of Passion	22

Later	23
Warmer Places	24
The Estate	25
A Table with a View	26

The Mysterious Woman Next Door

Feeding Crows	28
The Complacency of Fools	29
Roadside Disappointments	30
The Guardian of the Hourglass	31
Getting to Know Her	32
A Good Place to Bite	33
The Space between Breaths	34
Kiss Me	35
Looking for Tomorrow	36
Living Easy	37
The Trouble with Passion	38
Buying Knives	39
Waiting for Angels	40
Deliberate Departure	41
Chinese for Lunch	42
Ecology from the Stool	43
The Mysterious Woman Next Door	44
Ten Things to Say to a Naked Woman	45
Vampire Love	46
Advice from a Cynical Soul	47
The Neighbor's Cat	48

Joining the Demented

The Exhibit	50
The Report	51
An Old Man at the Beach	52
The First Days of Retirement	53
Joining the Demented	54
At the End of Frustration ...	55
The Bite	56
Observations ... Obsessive-Compulsive	57
It would take a very small Vampire	58

A Note in the Window

The Mad Moon	60
The Stonecutter's Balls	61
Connection with God	62
Sex with Old People	63
The Monsters	64
An Awkward Book Blurb	65
Hello, Goodbye	66
The Motive	67
A Note in the Window	68
A Lover's Lament	69
At the Shelter	70
Smoke Ring Halos	71
Ghost without Memories	72
The Mad Poet's Haiku	73

Of Public Safety	74
Breakfast with David	75
The Arsonist	76
The Future of History	77

Louisiana Calling

Louisiana Calling	80
And We Danced	81
Those Bright and Shiny Eyes	82
Mistaken for the Homeless	83
Sparrows in Flight	84
Gifts from the Far Side of the Moon	85
Confessing to a Suicide	86
The Death of Forgiveness	87
Calling in the Power Outage	88
Closing Shop	89
Hearts Don't Always Break	90
Showering in the Dark	91
Monkey Man Love	92
Todd and the Parrot	93
Power Outage – the Second Day	94
Church Girls	95
Love's Persistent Argument	96
A Pirate's Night Out	97
The Girl with the Pick Sock	98
After the Fire	99
A Note from Someone I Once Knew	100

The Fine Art of Poisoning

Decoding a Sacramento Night ...	102
The Long Run	103
Waiting for Angels	104
Spring	105
The Plague of the Politically Correct	106
Listening for Shadows	107
Flying over Texas	108
Every Morning	109
Blinking Skies	110
Waiting for God	111
The List	112
Orphaned Kisses	113
Machines of Loving Grace	114
Red Enameled Lips	115
The Getaway	116
The First Time	117
Realizing Lonely	118
The Contender	119
Tattoos, Coffee, a Small Cafe	120
You're in My Prayers	121
The House Next Door	122
Filling Out Forms	123
My Fourth of July in Idaho	124
Falling in Love	125
A Cat Named Kevorkian	126

Lipstick and Bullet Holes

Laughing at Funerals	128
Christ, I Love You – Bad	129
At 65	130
The Reemergence of Natural Law	131
Rented Rooms	132
From a Bar in Kansas	133
The Obscurity of it All	134
The Inside of Things	135
The Girl Upstairs	136
Hello to a Memory	137
The First Five Lines of a Blues Song	138
In the Moment I Said	139
A Sinister Mess	140
Looking at the Moon Alone	141
The Opera Critic	142
Mambo Partners	143
The Life of a Bubble	144
The Short History ...	145
The Battle of Champions	146
Meeting the Angels	147

The Mysterious Book of Old Man Poems

José Montoya	150
It's Late and I've been Drinking	151
Another Global Warming ...	152

Texas Fireflies	153
1949 Till Now	154
Lonely Light	155
Around the End of September	156
Chairs to Go	157
Ruby S. – the reincarnation of	158
Christmas Eve with Her	159
The Vocabulary of Movement	160
Going through Lists	161
The Sad Eyed Girl	162
A Lonely Love	163
A Birthday in San Antonio	164
The Reason for the Apology	165
The "WPA" Garden Work	166
The Late Hours	167
The Last Light of Summer	168
The Digging	169
The Screams of the Oleanders	170
A Bum in Reno	171
Something Got Past the Quality ...	172
An Afternoon Nap	173
A Coffee Shop on San Pedro	174
Kissing Shadows	175
The Music	176
Notes to a Dead Lover	177
Picking Up Beer Cans	178
A Magical Thing	179
The Absence of Charm	180
An Evening's Intrusion	181

New Poems

The Anonymous Poem	184
The Reason Old Men Shuffle	185
Little Monsters	186
Date Night	187
The Color of Paint	188
Gifts from Bella Lugosi	189
You Never Know	190
We Talked about Things	191
Molly's Funeral	192
How a Hitman Eats Spaghetti	193
Me and the Moon	194
Needing Wishes	195
A Tip for Hard Times	196
Keeping Dogs	197
Sunday's Family Potluck	198
Another Goodbye	199
The Lucky One	200
Dressing for Drinks and a Movie	201
Shaky Old Men and Upscale Joints	202
The End of Time	203
Dogs and Reptiles	204
Miles Away	205
What People Eat	206
A Quiet Turn Around	207
The Great Salami Famine	208

A True Story

Author's Notes:

When the folks at Spartan Press asked to do a book of selected poems, I jumped. My only question was – short poems? Their reply – yes. So, here we are, call them what you want: American Haiku, Minimal Poems, whatever. I prefer short poems – it's easy.

I have long believed the short poem is the hardest poem to write. The author must get in and get out, while saying something beyond a journal entry on the way. Yes, the short poem is written with intent, depth of thought, economy of words, and in the tightest of packages. Waste nothing. And that is A True Story.

– Bill

Roxy - 2003

Catching Knives
with Your Teeth

Kissing her
was like catching knives
with your teeth.

I knew
it was just a matter of time
before someone was hurt.

When I thought
I had mastered the game
she stopped
wiped her lip

with one finger

and said
"I think you're bleeding."

Coffee Shop Blues

He stared into his cup –
there was a wish being made.

He was looking for a friend –
no one offered.

Maybe a hand to shake –
none appeared.

So he sipped his rejection –
quietly

and poured himself –
into another
   empty night.

Separate Goals

She just wanted me
to touch her
softly.

I just wanted
to touch her
softness.

An Abbott and Costello Love Story

They are having
an Abbott and Costello marathon
on T.V.
I used to watch them
when I was young.
Now I watch them
when I'm old.
They still look the same
she says
I do too.

Memories of a Romance –
Gone Away

I love how your perfume
is there to greet me
even
if you're not.

The Touch

If
I could only touch
one place
I hoped
she would let me
touch her
there.

The Bookstore Clerk

I asked for William Carlos
Williams.
She said, "Who?"
I said, "The poet."
She said, "How do you spell it?"
I said, "What?"
She said, "Excuse me sir
I don't do literature
I do retail."

Ummm –

Walking into the coffee shop

she said,
"Ummm – smells nice."

I thought to myself
"Ummm – nice ass."

She said, "I bet it tastes good."

I said, "I bet it does."

Whispers in Public

She pointed
to the rose colored panties
and with a bashful grin
softly asked
"What do you think
of those?"
I leaned close
and whispered
"I think
they would look
beautiful
laying on the floor
next to our bed."

Anxiety's Bite

I whispered,
"I love you"
and waited
for her reply.

That New York Thing

She said,
"I cried in the car today."

I asked, "Why?"
She said, "That New York thing."

52 years
of guarding the gate
of holding the world back
and then
with one whisper
from her
I'm driven to my knees.

She said
"I cried in the car today."

It Might As Well
Been Written In Blood

She wrote in lipstick
on the bathroom mirror
"FUCK YOU
　I'M GONE."
Ten years of battling.
She won.

The Addict

The venom
of her passion
makes me
crave
another kiss.

The Gender Police

Not one
to hide
her emotions
they arrested her
when she
exposed
her heart.

She Answered

I asked why women
don't seem to write
with brutality.
She answered,
"Because
we live it."

Her Powder

Her powder
on the windowsill
next to the tub
left there
to remind me
of all the places
it's been
and all the places
I
will never go
again.

To Run With the Savages
2005

To Run With the Savages

Most are one or the other.
To run with the savages
you need to be both
mean
and tough.

Everything is met
with eyes focused
no conversation
no running to momma
no place to hide.

To survive
you need to learn
to take your meat
fresh.
Remember
they don't want to kill you
they want to eat you
alive.

The Contender

When I was a kid
you had to be
a contender.
The chances of becoming
a champ
were always slim
but if you stayed in the fight
long enough
a few
would leave you
alone
    it was always a surprise
        who they'd be.

The Visit

(for Paige Marie DePedro)

She's a little over a year old.
I could do the math
and tell you exactly
but I don't care
and neither does she.
She just messes with things
plays with her tongue a lot
yells at her sister –
   in that pre-language
   language
   that only little kids know.
Probably calling her a bitch.
I like that part
it's a sign of potential.
And they say man-eaters
aren't born that way –
   wait till she gets teeth.

Invitations
from the Jukebox

As it spilled
from the jukebox
   "There's going to be
    a heartache
    tonight"
she walked in
with those thin ankles
strapped into those
fuck me
pumps
pulling down
her sunglasses
so opportunity could see
those "Why wait
eyes?"

Someone asked for change
for the music
hoping to find
a less dangerous
invitation.

The Emergency of Passion

Zippers
are good
elastic
is best
buttons, hooks and clips
are a poor choice
but if it gets down to it
where
the emergency of passion
outweighs
the restraint of reason
just tear
and lick.

Later

Sometimes
I write poems
that scare her.
She reads them
before I get up
cries
after I leave
and tells me
about it
later.

Warmer Places

(for Kim and Bonnie)

For want of salt
she licked his neck
and dreamed
of Salty Margaritas
and someone named
Fernando
of hidden hideaways
warmer places
a beach in Mazatlan
with him.

When she woke
the house was cold
she tiptoed to the kitchen
held herself tight
pulled a chair close
and sat waiting
for the stove
to warm.

The Estate

I'm done.
I'm giving it all to the church.
The whole damn mess.
They can have it all
do what they want
keep it
sell it
I don't care.
Maybe get enough money
to buy some wine
throw a party
their choice.
I DON'T CARE.
The nuns can go through it
piece by piece
they might like
the porn collection.
At worst
they can use it
to teach the choirboys
what it takes
to make an angel
fly.

A Table with a View

I would have liked to have seen
a little more of her thigh
but her skirt only
slipped up so far
and she was too young
to show any more
and I was too old
to expect it.
But sometimes it's okay
to wish upon unopened
flowers.
To tip waitresses
a little more that you should.
Especially
when they give you
a table
with a view.

*The Mysterious Woman
Next Door
2008*

Feeding Crows

When the job
is done with me
when the hours
are once again
mine
I'm going to the park
to feed
the crows.
My kind of bird –
common
open with their
thievery.
I never have taken
to the pigeons
much.
A little too human
for me
beggars
without
tin cups.

The Complacency of Fools

They don't
frighten
the way they
should
not realizing
that age
has only
made us
look safe.

Roadside Disappointments

They do it all the time.
This one said
"FRESH LOCAL HONEY."
I stopped – inquired
it wasn't what I'd hoped.

The Guardian
of the Hourglass

It is his place
his job
his justification
for living
to choke off
everything
going up
and everything
coming down.
He is the guardian
of the hourglass
the guy in the middle.

Getting to Know Her

I told her to drop by sometime
bring fruit.
She showed up with a pomegranate.
You ever try to eat one of those things?
It's like
trying to suck the brains
out of a monkey
through an eye socket.
By the time the fighting's done
everybody's bloodied up –
you
the pomegranate
and the monkey.

We both learned things
about the other
we really didn't need to know
that night.
The next time she came by
she called first
was curious
if I liked
peaches.

A Good Place to Bite

I always liked
the soft part
of the thigh
the inside
just below
where the leg
and the body
come together.
It's a good place
to start
when considering
the tender meat.

The Space between Breaths

Reading her poem
I notice
the difference between
the words
"lovelies"
and "love lies"
is only
one small gap
a pause
no more
than the space
between
breaths.

Kiss Me

All the way
to the bottom
of you.
That's just how far
I can fall
into
a kiss
when you
kiss me.

Looking for Tomorrow

Windshield
dirty
truck
pushing
through time
hitchhikers
with signs
needing to be
someplace else.

This is not a rescue
it's an escape.
They can find
their own way.
The gas gauge
says
go.
So
we go.

Living Easy

Gave up the booze
just smoke dope
anymore.
I like the stuff
the Mexicans grow.
It takes you places –
heaven
sometimes.
The doctor
wrote a prescription
said it's a good thing
to have
when you're medicating
with angels.

The Trouble with Passion

One way
you forget to the load the gun
the other
you carry extra bullets
and depending on the mood
you'll either spend the morning
helping her
look
for a missing earring
in the crumpled sheets
or you're a suspect
sitting in the back seat
of the squad car.

That's the trouble with passion
you never know
which way
it's going to go
until the trigger
is pulled.

Buying Knives

I went to the internet
to buy a new knife
typed in stiletto
seven pairs
of pointy toed
spiked high-heels
came up.

I thought,
"Sharp."
Bought the ones
with the leopard skin
print.
Sent them to her
with a note
Don't cut yourself baby
but if you do
I'm here
to lick the wound.

Waiting for Angels

Haven't seen the angels
in a while
they must be
hiding out
probably know something
we don't
maybe something
we should.
In either case
I worry.

Deliberate Departure

Assisted Suicide –
She hates the name
tells me they should call it
something else.
Maybe –
    "Deliberate Departure"
says, "it isn't
what it is
Assisted Suicide."
Then offers
"But
I would help
you."

Chinese for Lunch

It's a mystery
why some insist
on using chopsticks.
Messing with their food
like that.

If you want to play
get a ball
if you want to eat
eat
if you want to impress me
then pickup
the check.

Ecology from the Stool

The solitary beasts
are the most vicious.
My advice
leave them
the fuck alone.

The Mysterious Woman Next Door

She's very clean.
Well
except for that time
she caught something.
We all noticed
the rash.
Other than that
she's very clean.

Ten Things to Say to a Naked Woman

Tell her
I love you
nine more
times.

Vampire Love

She looked like
she could have drank
a bucket of blood.
Instead
she took a sip
of mine.
What a night.
Oh – what a night.

Advice from a Cynical Soul

Learn to write the short poem
something you can read
while falling from a ten story
building.
Develop substance
learn to project.
It's advised
you have memorable material
when accompanied
by the oohs, ahs and screams
of the spectators.
It's not suggested
that there would be a push
but there are several among us
myself including,
who would freely volunteer
to unlatch the window
clear the pigeons from the ledge
and hold your wine glass
should you decide to jump.

The Neighbor's Cat

From my window
I saw it all.
The animal control people
didn't pick it up
neither did I.
The cars rolled by
some swerved
but most just
rolled by.
It just kept getting
flatter
and flatter
and flatter
until finally
if you didn't know it was there
you wouldn't notice the stain.
Yesterday
he stopped to ask
if I'd seen his cat.
I told him yes
it ran into the street
and just disappeared.

Joining the Demented
2009

The Exhibit

It was mostly sculptures
of female torsos
very nice.
No nipples though.
That might explain
why the place
was empty.

The Report

K. St. Marie is in bed
not sleeping
but trying to

and that Goddamn Alice
is on the couch
buried under the green blanket
putting out heat.

I spend my nights here
the TV talking loud
the computer thinking quietly
and the mini blinds closed tight.
I peek at the gay guy
next-door.

I suspect he knows more
about the disappearance
of my weenie dog
than he's telling.

I watch for clues
nothing yet.
He's good.

An Old Man at the Beach

The back
of her bikini
looked like
a little red
smile
covering
her butt.
I smiled back.
It was a private
moment
no one
noticed.

The First Days of Retirement

She called
wanted to know
what I was doing.
I told her
"Laying in bed
trying to levitate
been working on it
for hours
was getting close
now I gotta start
all over again."

Joining the Demented

I've always known
they were here
the monsters.
No one
believed me.
I kept it quiet
for the most part.

Now I see them
everywhere.
They still don't
believe me.
This is the last
I'll say
about it.

At the End of Frustration
the Mob Demanded

Give me a wand.
There are things
in need of change
and the only avenue
left
is magic.

The Bite

Something
bit my neck
It wasn't her.
I think maybe a spider.
It doesn't look like
any wound
she's left
before.

Observations of an Obsessive-Compulsive

The funeral went good
but the cemetery
was maddening
a jumble of headstones
nothing
in alphabetical
order.

I suspect
I was the only one
to notice.

It would take
        a very small Vampire

to find out
if a hummingbird's
blood
is sweet.

*A Note in the Window
2011*

The Mad Moon

It was there
last night
the moon
full and smiling.
But, tonight
nothing.

Somebody
must have said
something
pissed it off.

Now we got
another month
of fumbling
in the dark
hoping to bump
into each other

and it could
have been
so easy.

The Stonecutter's Balls

I want the inscription
on my headstone
to simply read
   "Beat Ya."

Actually
I want it to read
   "Beat Ya – now fuck off."

But I'm not sure
the stonecutter
has the balls
to go down
in immortality
with me
like that.

So, maybe
we should just put

"Fuck off."

Connecting with God

I do my praying
in the shower.
Seem to get better
reception there.

I'm feeling the need
now.
Join me.

It's a small shower
you can kneel
first.

Sex with Old People

When you
find the moist spot
there's a good chance
somebody peed.

The Monsters

They carry their knives
for other reasons
leave scars
in passing
it's a thing
they just
like to do
like carving
"I love you"
in a picnic table
only
with a little more
pain.

An Awkward Book Blurb

I like the cover.

Hello, Goodbye

I much prefer – hello
how you been
I've missed you.

Goodbye –
I'm always the last
to turn away
maybe
you haven't
noticed.

The Motive

She likes
that he does
her laundry
doesn't realize
he has
his favorites.

A Note in the Window

One leg reaching up
long, slender, thin ankle.
One foot
one toe
drawing a heart
in the condensation
putting a crooked arrow
through it
writing
goodbye love
backwards.

A Lover's Lament

Every time
I'm pushed
to the edge
ready to scream
"FUCK LOVE"
she walks in
and I think
if she smiles
I'll give it
one more
just
one more
chance
and
you do.

At the Shelter

Stooped
he carries
a pillow
as if it has
weight

defends it
as if it has
a porch
a doorbell
a lawn
to mow.

Smoke Ring Halos

"Hand me my shoes"
is all she says.
That's when
morning zippers
get left undone
when soft silk slips
peek
from uneven hems
when
shoe straps
get hung
from sleepy fingers
cigarettes
lit
get waved
in lazy salutes
when bare feet
touch
the hardwood
and car keys
jingle
when goodbye kisses
get blown to the night
and smoke ring
halos
follow her
out the door.

Ghosts without Memories

My father
never visits
in my dreams.
He's been gone too long
to miss me
and me
I've waited too long
to be missed.
So goes the ways
of dreams
and the hauntings
of ghosts
without memories.

The Mad Poet's Haiku

It is Fall, he thinks
of murdering the neighbor
for something to write.

Of Public Safety

Quit straightening the roads
this is America
we have a right to be crooked.

Breakfast with David
(for David Meltzer)

The waiter asked
if he could take his plate.
With the voice
of a Zen master
David replied
"I was leaving it for the flies
they look so hungry
besides
there's so many."

The Arsonist

There's that feeling
when sipping bourbon
the heat
when breathing
slow
out the nose
the burn
from just a push
of air.
Then, pulling in
deep
the warm
filling you
like the sun
eating at
a shadow
just a hint
of flame.

The Future of History

Everyone went back
to living
like it was the only
thing to do
left the memories
to the past
forgot about what
happened

as if
it never did.

Yesterday's
moments
tremble
knowing they are
the future
of our history

wishing
they weren't.

*Louisiana Calling
2013*

Louisiana Calling

Send a card when you get there.
I'll miss you till next time
then after that.

Until then
may all your dreams
need alibis.

Remember me –
 *the last one
 to say goodbye.*

And We Danced

Last night
the pillow
soft
gave up its
dreams
too easily.

Those Bright and Shiny Eyes

She has the weird eyes
it's like they point
in different directions
but you're not sure.
You want to ask
but instead
just stare
and smile back
when one of them
looks at you.

Mistaken for the Homeless

The lady at the street fair
offered us
a free sample of organic
dog food.
My companion replied
"No thanks
I've already eaten."
The lady blushed
we smiled
it was
a good day.

Sparrows in Flight

In the shape
of a sparrow
new leaves
hide
in the tangle
of the branches

they'll spend
the summer
before
taking flight.

Some may stay
a bit longer
depending on
how loud
autumn whispers.

Gifts from the Far Side
of the Moon

I'll take the wild dreams
the ones that send you
out
into the daylight
looking for witnesses.

Confessing to a Suicide

I've been practicing the note
so far
all I can come up with
is
It was me.

The Death of Forgiveness

I've waited
too long
for god
to apologize.

No more.

Calling in the Power Outage

A young woman
answered,
said she was sorry
twice
started crying.

Christ, they're good.

Closing Shop

The last thing I do
at night
is put my gun
on the mouse pad.

Don't worry
I have another one
on the nightstand.

Hearts Don't Always Break

The x-rays
were negative
nothing broke.
Still
you could put
your fingers
in the bullet hole
both sides.

Showering in the Dark

To conserve energy
I've started showering
in the dark.
We could save twice
as much
if you
joined me.
Don't worry
about not being able
to see
I have an excellent
sense of touch
I'll find you.

Monkey Man Love

With her on top
it was one
of those primal
screams

the kind that sucks
the air
out of the room.

She put
her hand
over my mouth

and with
a warm-breathed
whisper
said
"Quiet
you'll wake
the kids."

Todd and the Parrot

He didn't used to
but he does now
drinks with the parrot
and the parrot
well
he's started to swear
says *shit* and calls people
motherfuckers.
He says the parrot baits him too
starts arguments
seems to win most.
If he knew it was going to be
like this
he would have left it
the way it was
and let the parrot
drink alone.

Power Outage – the Second Day

The Pad
my last link to the outside world
power out
a second day
batteries getting low
we're living like savages here
the gods have abandoned us.

Church Girls

The girls
coming from church
look like hookers
maybe
they're just
starting early.

Love's Persistent Argument

Always comes down to
who's going to sleep
on the wet spot?

A Pirate's Night Out

He came to read his poems.
We came to listen.

He brought an ex-girlfriend.
The one who tore up his house

>broke all the windows
>popped all the light bulbs
>scared his parrot
>wrecked his truck.

The one
he bought the knife
for.

He never even said – arrrr
like pirates do.

Still,
the crowd
sat on edge.

He thought
it was his poems.

The Girl with the Pink Sock

She carries
her cell phone
in a pink
sock.
Says it's her
weapon
of choice.
Learned it watching
old
prison movies.
Says it's better
than a bar
of soap
and the *Screws*
if they notice
just think it's
cute.

After the Fire –

we'll sweep the ash
wash the dogs
water down the porch
think about church
won't go
the kids and the neighbors
won't call.
We'll probably throw
a bale of hay out for the deer
some birdseed
for the wild ones
wonder when they're going
to get the power back up
and wait for the smoke to settle.
We'll think about how quiet it gets
without leaves.
It's always quiet
without leaves.

A Note from Someone
I Once Knew

He sent pictures
recovered from the fire
that took his sister.

I thanked him
politely
touched the delete button
softly

left his memories
where they
belong.

*The Fine Art of Poisoning
2013*

Decoding a Sacramento Night – the Saint of 24th St.

The guy
in the electric wheel chair
stops mid-block
rolls a joint
lets the smoke drift into
the fractured shadows
of an evening moon.

At the next intersection
he ignores the light.

The leaves piled
in the gutter –
he smiles
as they part
for him.

The Long Run

The phone rang late.
Everyone knows
I stay up
late.
Often – it was him
crazy drunk
an old friend.
We'd talk about
who we used to be
avoid
who
we've become.
A letter arrived
a few days back
said he died.
None of the usual stuff
when, where and how.
Just that
he died.
He'd been a dope fiend
for years.
It looks like
it finally got him.
It's love, loss
and time
that are taking me
at least
it looks like
they're catching up.

Waiting for Angels

Haven't seen the angels
in a while
they must be
hiding out
probably know something
we don't
maybe something
we should.
In either case,
I worry.

Spring

By the end of winter
most of the beer cans
will be gone
picked up and recycled
for cigarette money.
The yard
should be
safe
to mow.

The Plague of the Politically Correct

All I can offer is,
they're easily pissed off
to paraphrase Disney
"Six out of seven
midgets
agree."

Listening to Shadows

I heard your shadow last night
felt it pass me in the hall
heard your car start
pull out of the drive
and go.
Your chain – the St. Christopher
is still on the night stand.
There's a pair of stockings, shoes
I left them where they dropped.
The note
you taped to my rearview
it's still there.
I know
I can't help it
I miss you.
I'll leave the door unlocked
and a window open
just in case
your shadow
still loves me.

Flying Over Texas

I looked for you
when we flew over
Texas

but you must have been inside
sitting on that corner stool
legs jack-knifed,
talking those sweet things
to that other guy
the lucky bastard.

Miss you, love you
think about you
a lot
even at
30,000 feet.

Every Morning –

on my way in
I pass the guy
walking his Scotties
one black
one white.
I nod a hello.

With their leashes
in one hand
he raises the other
two fingers up
not quite in a peace sign
and waves
a bag of shit
at me.

Blinking Skies

The lights
of the gathering enemy
fill the skies.

We see stars
let our hearts ring
romantic
believe
the myths.

They
prepare
for the siege.

Waiting for God

The old man
is trying to die.
He's never done it
before
it's taking
awhile.

He's finding death
a friendly sort
likes to visit
hangout with the living
forgets
what he's here for.

In the hallway
someone whispers
"God will be here
soon enough."
No one prays.

The old man
stares at the ceiling
tells me
where he hid
his wedding ring.

The List

For their sake
I hope I never hear
the diagnosis
"You only have
six months
to live."

There are scores
to settle
grudges
to be made right
favors to return
lessons to teach.

When the end
has its date
consequence
begins to mean
less.
The penalty
has already been
levied.

I have a list
you may be
on it.

Orphaned Kisses

I should have stayed
longer
instead
I left early
with regret.

We only shared
three kisses.

On the way home
I wondered
how many
were left –
behind.

Machines of Loving Grace
(thanks to Richard Brautigan)

I worked the factories
a long time
owed no one there
nothing
gave them less
but the machines
had me
them I loved.
They never lied
still don't.

Red Enameled Lips

I found a pair
of red enameled
lips
on my nightstand
this morning.
Put them in a jar
for
safekeeping.
If you lost them
call me.
Then again
if they are
yours
I might want to
keep them
just a little
longer.

The Getaway

The hot air balloon
sat in waiting
one release of the knot
and they were gone.

When asked
which way they went
the witness replied
"Up."

The First Time

Last night
last night
you got lost
in that last kiss
didn't you?

I saw it
in your eyes
in the way
you had to look
to the streetlights
to catch your breath
in the way
you had to untangle
your feet
just to walk away.

How long
has it been
or was that
the first time
you've tried
to keep a secret
from yourself.

Realizing Lonely

The trouble
with growing old
is
you run out
of wishes.

The Contender

When I was a kid
you had to be
a contender.
The chances of becoming
a champ
were always slim
but if you stayed in the fight
long enough
a few
would leave you
alone –
it was always a surprise
who they'd be.

Tattoos, Coffee, a Small Cafe

She took
the window seat
back to the glass.
The passers by
enjoyed
the rose tattoo
the other cheek
unblemished
lovely as well.

You're in My Prayers

If certain people
would just die
life would be
okay.

The House Next Door Died

After
the new people
moved in
the weeds
found their way
the curtains grayed
and the chimney
called for a new pope.

Their kids
never come out
to play.

On quiet nights
you can hear
what's left
of the azaleas
weep.

Filling Out Forms

She'll be 81 April 21st.
It seems like her history
is mostly mine anymore.

The dementia has her
she sees things
that are worrisome
tells me I look like someone
she used to know
maybe one of her
sons
but older.

The lady at the home says
I need to think about
making
arrangements –
the Neptune Society
has a nice package.
Says she can help
with the forms
if I want.

On the way home
in the car
alone
I felt like
I was plotting
a murder.

My Fourth of July in Idaho

They sell mortar size fireworks
for personal use
here.
People shoot them off
in their front yards.

On the Fourth
the sky is lit 360 degrees
the noise makes it sound
like a war zone
the smell of gunpowder
takes me back
to my youth.

The morning paper
is quick to report
not a finger or eyeball
was lost
no houses burned.

On the fifth
all that's left
is to pick up
the beer bottles
and figure out
whose car
is parked in your
driveway.

I love it.

Falling in Love

Dark hair
dark eyes
and that skin.

Yeah, I fall in love
a lot
she's just the latest
not to know.

A Cat Named Kevorkian

The bird stood on the ledge
threatening to jump.
The cat paced below
hoping to assist
in the suicide.

Lipstick and Bullet Holes
2014

Laughing at Funerals

Joy comes
at the most
awkward
of moments.
I don't fight it
anymore.

Christ, I Love You - Bad

It's Valentine's Day.
I'm feeling like
we need to blow
something up.

After all
what's love
without the
flames
a boom,
and a few
sparkles?

At 65

In a few days
it's here
another birthday.
Most of them spent
trying to become
a legend.
It's taking longer
than I figured.

I'm tired.

The Reemergence of Natural Law

If you look tasty
you will be eaten.

Rented Rooms

We lie
scrambled

hot, tangled
everything
moist

the quivering
wreckage
of a spent
passion

trying to catch
our breath

before they come
to make
the bed.

From a Bar in Kansas City

I'm in a bar
in Kansas City
having a burger
a drink.
It's cold here
18 degrees outside.

I'm reading poems
across town
a little later.

Just wanted
you to know
no matter how far
or cold
it gets
you'll be
keeping me
warm
tonight.

Missing you
lots
from a Bar
in Kansas City.

The Obscurity of it All

The girl with the prosthetic leg
gained a little weight
her prosthetic didn't.
Looked a bit odd
just enough
that you
noticed.

The Inside of Things

People are not just
black or white.
If you've ever
peeled one
you'd know.

The Girl Upstairs

On the floor above
I hear her heels
click.
When the lights
are down
I can look up
see all the things
she tries to hide.

Hello to a Memory

Everybody
weeps
for somebody
dead.

I got a few tears
for you.
So
hurry up.

The First Five Lines
of a Blues Song

He wanted to write
a blues song
then found her note.

She wrote it
for him.

A Sinister Mess

When shooting crows
it quickly becomes
a sinister mess.

They gather in mass
gawking
demanding answers
to their mocking
questions
"Why? Why? Why?"

It's something
I choose
not to get
involved with
anymore.

I suggest
you
avoid
the murder
too.

In the Moment I Said

Tell me a secret kid.
I just need to know
you have one.

Her lips moved
quiet like.
I think she said
"I love you."

Looking at the Moon Alone

How much is lost
before realizing
there's no victory
in being the last
to weep.

The Opera Critic

In the morning
she puts the disc in the player
turns the volume
low.

Opera
not understanding the language
her whispers
most erotic
sung in an Italian accent.

She says the sound of his voice
makes the hair
at the base of her spine
tingle.

The little
blonde ones.

Mambo Partners

The wind blew its fingers
through the leaves of a willow
and whispered
"Hey Baby
care to dance?"

The Life of a Bubble

She pushed
a little pink
bubble
from between her lips
then seeing me
see her
pulled it back
popped it behind
a blush and a grin.

It lasted
just
that
long
the little
pink bubble.

The Short History of the Development of Man

It started out slow
then just went
fucking crazy.

The Battle of Champions

He's been relegated
to walking the dog
a nasty little creature
who terrorizes small children
and garden reptiles.
It's a tough job
for someone who once
ran
with the champions.
Now
every day he slips
farther from the fight
the edge keeps wearing
smooth
until finally
the calluses are gone
and the only battle felt
is with the meanness
and the thought
of letting that damn dog
chase a wet tennis ball
into the traffic.

Meeting the Angels

It doesn't matter
who you are
we all believe
we'll be forgiven
move to Heaven
smoke dope
with the angels
never get fat.

If it's not there
Heaven
the worry
was for nothing.

I still like wearing
my crucifix
Saint Christopher
and the silver chain.

If nothing else
it's kept the vampires
away
makes me feel
like I'm
part
of something
like I belonged
even if with

just the outcast.

*The Mysterious Book
of Old Man Poems
2017*

José Montoya

While visiting
D Street
he pointed to my beard – said

*You're turning chrome man
becoming an elder.
Don't worry
you'll be alright.*

It's Late and I've been Drinking

I'm sitting here
messing around
minding my own
business.
Out of the corner of my eye
I see the cat.
Then I hear the dog
bark.
Well, not really a bark
something more like burr
maybe kind of like a barff
short and low
quiet like
more just to get
my attention
than anything.
The truth is
we don't have a cat.
It's late
and I've been drinking.
Regardless
I'm glad the dog
saw it too.

Another Global Warming Talking Point

Nipples
hard.

Even
in this heat
she still turns
heads.

Texas Fireflies

You saw them?
I'm jealous.
Did you let out a gentle
sigh
lean in
to someone
a little closer?
Set your iced tea down
leave a cool evening kiss
on a warm cheek?
Fireflies
do that
to people
at least
they should.

1949 Till Now

The year I was born
the rubble of war
lingering
the great machines
being tore down
repurposed
sold for scrap
their DNA still pulsing
in the automobiles
trucks, tanks
bombs
the spoon
that dips
my evening soup.

Lonely Light

In his room
alone
he bleeds light
not enough to bother
the neighbors
but enough
to attract the moths
for the cat
to play with.
Enough
to keep him up
late
write poems by.
Enough
to make him wish
he wasn't so
goddamned lonely.

Around the End of September

A different kind
of warm
settles in.
Not too hot
the sticky gone.
It's nice.
I like it
we can sleep
close.

Chairs to Go

Saw a guy
walking downtown
carrying a chair
a kitchen chair
he was carrying it
like a surfboard
except with legs
you know.
I imagine
he's ordering them
the chairs
one at a time
to go.

Ruby S. – the reincarnation of

Saw your picture
in the obits.
Christ, you were beautiful.
I could have loved you
but we missed
each other
time
place
circumstance.
It all runs together.
Maybe next time?
I'll keep an eye open
ask around
now
that I know
what you look like.

Christmas Eve with Her

No cooking prep
no mistletoe hanging
no rum drinks to set a mood.
Just the continuing drone
of knives being sharpened
coming from the kitchen.
Lots of knives.

The Vocabulary of Movement

Modern dance
an acquired taste.
At the end
of the performance
all I could think
was
those girls
really need
to wash
their feet.

Going through Lists

They send email
reminders
of people's birthdays.
When I go through the list
all that comes to mind is
Christ, you're still alive.

The Sad Eyed Girl

She quit shaving
her eyebrows
looks like Frida
now
except
with short hair
and boy's shoes.
She's convinced
nobody loves her
him, her
nobody.
You want to ask
if anyone's
touched it
yet
but you don't.
Still
for her sake
you hope
someone has.

A Lonely Love

One room
a kitchenette
and a bath.
Six-fifty a month
her secret place
where she keeps
the little things
the memories
one chess piece
a little silver happy-face
drawn on its side –
a pill bottle
three lipstick
stained
cigarette butts
inside
the lid tight
a pillow to hold
when she's lonely
it smells like
someone else
and the corner of the bed
where she sits
rocks herself
and wishes
just wishes.

A Birthday in San Antonio

Yeah, it's been a while.
Still missing you
lots.
That won't stop
no matter how many
birthdays go by.

You still wear that
red lipstick?
It's your color.
I can see you
blowing out the candles
now.

Make a wish kid
something big.
I got mine
you're in it.
Happy Birthday
to you.

The Reason for the Apology

I just wanted you
to shut the fuck
up.
Not go away
and die
or anything.
Just
shut the fuck
up.

The "WPA" Garden Work

Left the window open last night
the crickets were talking
hadn't heard them in a while.
They acted like they knew me.
I said, *Hey-man*, asked how long
they'd be working.
One of them answered
We're pulling a Graveyard
tonight man.
I thought about closing the window
but didn't want to be rude.
One of them asked, *Why?*
I said, *Nothing man, nothing.*
It was quiet for a minute
then everybody went back to work.
I slept on the couch
they were gone this morning.
Tonight,
it was just the clean up crew.

The Late Hours
(for D.R. Wagner)

Read your poems this morning
they brought the magic
left me smiling.
I imagine
in the late hours
your rooms fill
with mysterious visitors
and odd creatures
on wondrous
adventures.
I am always thankful
they enjoy your company
leave you
with a bit of something
to talk about.

The Last Light of Summer

The weather
finally starting to turn
but with the fires and all
the sun still casts
its orange shadows.
Gives an old man
uneasy feelings.
Been through it before.
The trees in the back
still show their scars.
Mine
they're a bit harder to read
especially this time of year
with my heavy coat
and dark pants.
Grief likes to keep its
secrets warm.
Like most old men
I hide mine.

The Digging

I've taken up
a new pastime
digging
in the back.
Moving this pile
to that pile
and that pile
to the other pile.
Sometimes
I make a new pile.
Most days Kae St. Marie
comes out
says
I have a cold drink
for you.
You might want to
come in
before it gets too hot.
Some days I do
some days I don't
depends
on the digging.
She says
people ask about me.
She tells them
It keeps him home
off the bourbon
and he seems
to enjoy it
the digging.

The Screams of the Oleanders

The Oleanders
have once again
been butchered.
Their skeletal remains
a tribute to my mastery
of residential yard care.

A Bum in Reno

With a voice
gentle
he asked if I had a dollar.
I gave him two.

Then about the dime
pointed
said, *You dropped it*.
I said, *Yeah*.

Thanks
not much of a word.
He said it twice
his eyes
once more.

I told him
Be safe man.

He said
It's hard.

Something Got Past
the Quality Control People

There was something floating
in the Top Ramen.
Not sure what it was
a sample
a mistake
a test marketing ploy
a piece of a finger?
Regardless
I ate it.

An Afternoon Nap

The flight didn't really
last that long
but there was that moment
that one moment
when it felt like the sky
had no bottom.
Looking down
blue, gray, a mist of pink
there was nothing to see
no birds, dust, leaves blowing
just me, for a moment free
from whatever it is
chains us
to ourselves.

A Coffee Shop on San Pedro

Iced tea
and yoga pants.
One gets me
in the door
the other
keeps me there.

And oh yeah –
the company
of strangers.

But
if you want to
place a bet
go with
the yoga pants.

Kissing Shadows
(for A.M., 3/30/1936 - 7/9/2016)

Under the hum
of a tired Sacramento
air-conditioner
we said goodbye.
I kissed her shadow
she kissed mine.
We both knew
whatever time does
however dark
it gets
we may never again
but our shadows
always will
find
one another.

The Music

She reached over
dimmed the music
said, *I couldn't hear
you breathe.*

Notes to a Dead Lover

She sends notes
into the ether
apologies to a dead
lover
sorry you missed
so much living
today was special
someone kissed me
I think
you would have liked him.

Picking Up Beer Cans

Feeling better today
still a bit fuzzy
don't want to
kill anyone
though.
Yesterday
I did.
Today
I'm good.

A Magical Thing

She told me
always embrace
to the left.
That way
you're heart
to heart.
And if you hold
tight enough
and long enough
the beats become
one.
Said it is a magical
thing.
Asked
if I wanted to try?
Said the secret is
to never
let go.

The Absence of Charm

Since
the bookstore cat
Romeo
died
no one says
watch the door
don't let the cat
out – please.

Even though
I seldom
saw the cat
and I still don't
I wish they would
say it.

Seems
such a charming way
to let the world know
you've come
you've gone.

An Evening's Intrusion

On the porch
wishing a cigarette
the first sip
of bourbon
he looks
a bit younger
with the second
at peace.
It's his eyes.

The neighbor lady
Ruth
widowed a decade
from her porch
waves.
He waves back.

The street lights
stagger to life
hide the sky.
One by one
the stars go out.

New Poems

The Anonymous Poem

Tonight
that's all I got
six lines
of a skinny poem
not even
a title.

The Reason Old Men Shuffle

Murderer
yes, I know.
A lifetime spent
killing
invisible gods.

Who knew
there are so many?
Their corpses scattered
everywhere
the reason old men
shuffle

trying to avoid
tripping
but still
now and then
we do.

Little Monsters

If you hang out
in the yard long enough
the lizards
start staring.
It's fucking creepy.

Date Night

We had red meat
tonight.
Prime Rib
and the other
stuff
all the other
stuff.
14 ounces
we ate about ten
each
and the other
stuff
all the other
stuff.
Took the rest
home
dogs
and sandwiches.
Our bloodlust
complete.

The Color of Paint

Painted the shed
a deep forestry brown
so in the dark
it disappears.

Tonight, it's gone.

If this works
as planned
in the morning
it will be returned.

If not
we lost
another one.

Gifts from Bella Lugosi

Thought I saw it
asked.
She said
a goddamn bat
get it.
Rose and Mrs. Menebroker
the dogs
thought it was
great fun
bouncing on the bed
to short
to get any altitude.
I broke the upstairs'
window screen
getting it off
hurrying
the little bastard's
escape.
He shit on the wall
on the way out.

You Never Know

The kid in line
looked shifty.
I didn't trust him.

Asked me to sign
his book.
I figured
he was – up to
something.

These days
things happen.
You never know.

No sense
taking a chance.
I forged
my name.

We Talked about Things –
it didn't Help

My barber's wife
is dying.
It was the saddest
haircut
ever.

Molly's Funeral

I'll sit in the car
wait for you.
Sip a little bourbon
take a little
nap.
We'll drive home
slow
talk about
something else.

How a Hitman
Eats Spaghetti

I like my marinara
with bow tie pasta.
You don't have to
fuck around
getting it on the fork
just stab it once
and it's done.

Me and the Moon

The moon is quiet
doesn't want to talk
tonight.
I'll just crawl off
to bed
pretend I don't hear them
(the wind and the rain)
taunting me.
Wait for another
tomorrow
search the skies
for a whisper
we'll talk then.
Me and the moon.

Needing Wishes

The wish –
a delicate wrist
small, thin
one deserving
of its own
fragrance
and silver bangles
worn late
into the morning.
Let them jingle
when she wakes.
There are other things
needing wishes
too.
We'll just start here.
Move on later.

A Tip for Hard Times

A bag of thrift-store
paperbacks
one dollar
twenty – thirty titles.
Cut the covers off
use them for postcards
they're just the right size.
Postage, thirty-five cents.
You may have to
shorten them up
an inch or so
just cut 'em straight.
And try to be selective
sending *Mommy Dearest*
for your Mom's birthday
could be awkward.

Keeping Dogs

She likes to have a dog
in the house.

Says she needs
someone
something
to listen
to talk to
to sit with
and hold.

I told her,
I'm here
for you baby.

She just smiled.

Sunday's Family Potluck

The gravy
is weak
and the bourbon
thin.
Still, both help
to cut the taste
of Uncle Frank's
scalloped potatoes.

Another Goodbye

They took a tooth
today.
A molar
way back
in the back.
At my age
I guess I can
afford
to lose one.
Still it was an old
friend.
Lots of red meat
bacon
sourdough
dipped in blood
egg yoke
bourbon
and Harvey Wall Bangers
pasted its way.
My guess –
a few hundred pounds
worth.
It was a good tooth.
I'll miss it.

The Lucky One

It's late
time for bed.
I got monsters
wanting for me.
I wish they'd love
somebody else.
But, I'm always
the lucking one.
Who do you thank
for that?

Dressing for Drinks
and a Movie

Just wear the pearls.
You don't need
nothing else
baby.
Not with me.
Just the pearls.

Shaky Old Men and
Upscale Joints

He held his drink
with two hands.
One for the glass
the other
for the straw –
never raised it
off the table.

When they brought
the second
he had to up-cycle
the straw.

Move it from
one glass
to the other.
The cheep
bastards.

The End of Time

There will be a whisper
then something
a little louder
then the silence
the denying
the face saving
until one of them
finally ask –
What have
we done?

Dogs and Reptiles
(Spring 2020)

Had to go out last week
get the dogs their
rattlesnake vaccinations.
Lock-down or not
the snakes are still out.

Miles Away

Knuckles hurt
back hurts too.
Everything fucking hurts.
It's who I am.

Then there's the cute picture
on a Christmas card
Kae St. Marie and the kids
me –
looking innocent.

There are times
when all you can do
is look
smile
and let the wish
take you miles way
from who you are.
While trying
not to blink.

What People Eat

My mother was Irish
we ate potatoes
a lot of potatoes.
I still do.

A Quick Turnaround

Some guy
sent a friend request.
I said okay.
Just to be safe
I decided to send him
a message
"You better not be
a Commie rat."
I guess he was.

The Great Salami Famine

THE GREAT GALLO DRY SALAMI
FAMINE OF 2020 is finally over.
Our secret source has come through.
$9.99 for a 32 ounce cub in paper
wrap.
We got two
smuggled then out to the car,
then into the house.
Don't want the neighbors
hanging around
doing the poor me thing.
Don't ask where, it's top secret.
Unless you want to take a
blood oath.
Delicious.
I say no more.

Bill Gainer is a storyteller, humorist, poet, and a maker of mysterious things. He earned his BA from St. Mary's College, and his MPA from the University of San Francisco. He is the publisher of the PEN Award winning R. L. Crow Publications, and is the ongoing host of Red Alice's Poetry Emporium (Sacramento, CA). Gainer is internationally published, and known across the country for giving legendary fun filled performances. His work is not for sissies. Visit him in his books, at his personal appearances, or at his website: billgainer.com.